MW00416037

2011 GLOBAL POETRY ANTHOLOGY

2011

Global Poetry Anthology

~

Montreal International
Poetry Prize

EDITED BY

Valerie Bloom, Stephanie Bolster,
Frank M. Chipasula, Fred D'Aguiar,
Michael Harris, John Kinsella,
Sinéad Morrissey, Odia Ofeimun,
Eric Ormsby, and Anand Thakore

Signal
EDITIONS

SIGNAL EDITIONS IS AN IMPRINT OF VÉHICULE PRESS

SIGNAL EDITIONS EDITOR: CARMINE STARNINO

Cover design: David Drummond
Set in Filosofia and Minion by Simon Garamond
Printed by Marquis Book Printing Inc.

Montreal International Poetry Prize
www.montrealprize.com

LIBRARY AND ARCHIVES CANADA CATALOGUING IN PUBLICATION

Global poetry anthology : 2011 Montreal International Poetry Prize.

ISBN 978-1-55065-318-2

1. English poetry--21st century. 2. Canadian poetry (English)—
21st century.

PR9086.G56 2011   821'.9208   C2011-908448-1

Published by Véhicule Press, Montréal, Québec, Canada
www.vehiculepress.com

Distribution in Canada by LitDistCo
www.litdistco.ca

Distributed in the U.S. by Independent Publishers Group
www.ipgbook.com

Distributed in the U.K. by Gazelle

Printed in Canada on 100% post-consumer recycled paper.

Contents

Preface

THE POEMS IN THIS ANTHOLOGY are new, previously unpublished works from around the world, selected by a team of editors from Australia, Canada, Guyana, India, Ireland, Jamaica, Malawi, Nigeria, the U.K., and the U.S. We're happy to offer what may be the first chance most readers have had to read an anthology of global poetry, representing the rhythms, flavours, preoccupations and tastes of a diverse, international collection of poets writing in English.

The poems were selected "blind" (that is, the editors did not know the authors' names), allowing new voices to compete equally with established ones. As a result, work by emerging poets like Talya Rubin, John Wall Barger and Emeka Okereke sits comfortably side by side with poems by C.K. Stead, Robert Wrigley, Patricia Young and Adil Jussawalla. To reflect this emphasis on the poem itself, we have arranged them alphabetically by title.

As one might expect, given the open nature of the selection process, this anthology includes a wide array of poetic styles and interests. The lyric, the anecdotal, the monologue, the surrealist, the prose poem and the shape poem are all represented herein. Images, of course, are plentiful and diverse, while some motifs, like "eye" and "water," lend this anthology a feeling of unity.

As this is an annual anthology of new poetry, in some ways it may be taken as a snapshot of subjects that poets around the world were grappling with in 2011. The poems engage with a variety of concerns, including nature, the environment, history, race, religion and immigration. There is a recurring theme of mortality and suffering, on both domestic and national scales, which lends many of these poems urgency.

Putting together a global anthology of this kind would have been nearly impossible even five years ago. The growing ubiquity of the internet was necessary to bring all these editors and poets together from their far-flung countries, and to coordinate their participation.

We hope to be able to produce this anthology annually, bringing poets from various communities together to read each other's work, to hear each other's voices, and to engage with each other's diverse interests. It is our dream that this anthology will mark a fundamental moment in the exploration of the still nascent idea of "global poetry." And we hope that you will enjoy considering and perhaps debating the relative virtues of this twenty-first-century approach to literature. Go little book.

Peter Abramowicz
Asa Boxer
Len Epp

About the Montreal Prize

THE NONPROFIT Montreal International Poetry Prize was founded in 2010 with two goals in mind: to produce an annual anthology of previously unpublished poetry from around the world, and to deliver a major, annual, crowd-funded poetry award. In an important sense these two goals are symbiotic: the $50,000 prize provides an incentive to poets to enter their best work for selection in the anthology, and the prize is in turn funded directly by the poets who participate in the project. This dual nature is also reflected in the structure of our selection process: the ten editors select poems for the global poetry anthology, and the prize judge selects the prize-winning poem from those published in the anthology.

Significantly, our community-funding model inverts the ancient and venerable tradition of patronage funding for major literary awards. With the advent of the internet, poets and poetry lovers can now create major literary awards directly by building a global community of individual supporters. This is especially salient in an era of fiscal and economic recession, which is bound to impact all of the arts, poetry not least among them.

Our explicit commitment to "global poetry" is a deliberate response both to the opportunity for global reading presented by the internet, and to the deeply entrenched national or regional divisions usually applied to literature. We're not yet sure what "global poetry" or "global reading" will mean, as the world becomes increasingly inter-connected, but we do know it's the right time to introduce annual global anthologies of literature.

The Montreal Prize is also the first major literary award to be based on a "blind" judging process. This means that the identity of the poet is not directly at stake in the selections made by our editors or our prize judge. For those interested in literary theory, this raises some pertinent issues, which we encourage you to interrogate. For those interested in writing poetry, this means that ours is a flat or fundamentally democratic structure. First-time poets and Nobel laureates are equally welcome to enter their work, and are naturally subject to the same discrimination.

For more information about the Montreal International Poetry Prize, and to show us your support, please visit our website at www.montrealprize.com.

Acknowledgements

THIS ANTHOLOGY was made possible through the efforts of a great many people around the world. Each of them devoted much of their time, energy, creativity, and insight to our efforts to launch a global poetry project, and to bring it to fruition in a relatively short period of time.

Along the way, there were many people who met with us, pointed us in new directions, and gave us their general support, each of whom we do not have space to thank here. To all of you, we would like to say that your participation will always be a part of the history of this project, and whatever future it might have.

In particular, we would like to thank the following people for their support: Carolyn, Gabriel, Greg and Michael Harris; Sarah Abramowicz; Ben Okri; Don Paterson; Julie Keith and Richard Pound; Jeet Thayil; Helen Fotopulos; Robert Ladouceur; Simon Dardick and everyone at Véhicule Press; Shreya Jalali; Leigh Kotsilidis; Lucinda Tang; Mirka Snyder Caron; Carmine and Jennifer Starnino; Anita Lahey; David-Antoine Williams; Matt Huculak; Nick Brunt and Ian Conrad; Eric Benzacar; David Drummond; Alison Chote; and those of our families and friends who have endured us during this time.

We would also like to thank the members of our 2011 editorial board. It was very generous, and indeed courageous, for them to lend their support when this anthology and the Montreal Prize were mere gleams in the eye. Their early participation was crucial to making this project a reality. You can read their short biographical blurbs elsewhere in this anthology.

To the anonymous donors who also made this possible, we cannot thank you enough.

And finally, we would like to thank everyone who participated in the 2011 Montreal International Poetry Prize. You came together from all over the globe to form a new kind of poetry-funding com-munity, and believed in our vision for a poet-funded prize and an annual anthology of previously unpublished, global poetry. Without your participation, this anthology would not exist.

After Cancer

And there they were
just under the surface of the water,
full of the meat of the body, taut and silver,
liquid with grace,

what I asked for
when I asked to feel again
my own breath.
In the quiet of night,
you beside me dreaming,
I attend to the cathedral of my body,
its scarred and saddened walls,
and what I thought scarce, even vanished,
swims beside me
shark-finned, salmon-eyed,
intent on feeding whatever comes their way,
and I've learned not to run to the thinning shore
but stand among them breathing;

and when still I can't sleep
I think of all the sleepless others
stepping in beside me.

LESLIE TIMMINS

Aluminum Beds

When he pulls up in a truck and hefts new beds
into the house to replace our camp cots,
we see the dark in a metal's dull sheen
is the dark displayed in his beard. The sound
rushing through the hollows of the square posts,
the frames, guards and rails, is the sound rushing
through the spaces he has made within us.
He sets them all down, the pieces he measured,
sheared, and welded together in the evenings
in his father's factory, while I, half hidden
in among the machines, gathered up scrap
fallen to the cement floor. The four beds
stand in our shared room, one for each of us—
with this he fulfills his unwanted office.
He leaves us soon after, and I keep vigil.
Nightly I allow not one of my brothers
to speak or even audibly breathe. I know
that the sound of any of our young voices
will distract the light trying to make its way
through the fitted substance of the metal. I know
at the same time that this light is my father
searching for his sons. He does not know it—
long before he left us, his love began travelling
to us apart from him. If I memorize him,
I will be able to see the love. If I cut
from myself all that is not my love for him,
the right set of rays will find us. My brothers
fall asleep one by one. I lie and wait
for my dream. There is no space not swirling,
no fire with its core of blackness not burning,
within the beds' angular emptiness
because of the love meant for us. Through the night,
the metal embraces me. It is a skeleton,

unending silver, pure and cold, and I become it,
the light of my father's love arrived at last.

RUSSELL THORNTON

Among Schoolchildren

For Father Edmund Harris

The one-story houses were painted aqua, violet, orange, pistachio.
I spoke to the taxi driver in broken Spanish.
I was becoming a priest, I told him, God willing,
as we drove over muddy ruts, pot holes, and alongside hungry dogs.
Much of the taxi's interior had been removed.
Time slowed that summer in San Pedro Sula.
Around the rotary, legless men shook their tambourines,
epileptics convulsed and the blind tapped their sticks
through donkey excrement. Blue mountains and fields of banana trees
shadowed the city's edges. There were the many poor
on the muddy river bank assembling huts out of rubbish.
I had come to work in an orphanage in Villa Florencia.
Inside the ten foot wall with barbed wire, behind the metal gate,
guards fingered their pistols like bibles,
and seventy orphaned girls politely greeted strident Christians.
One had been found on a coconut truck.
She had lived on coconut juice since birth,
had trouble speaking, preferred not to be held.
Two sisters had been left at a street corner on a sheet of cardboard;
their mother told them to wait, then never came back.
It was a landscape both porous and uninviting.
Half way up one mountain was an enormous white Coca-Cola sign.
Rain steadily fell against the tin roofs and colored the chapel windows to plum.
Sweat colored my T-shirt the color of a steeped tea-bag.
At night, grease on my cheeks shone, lit by the Coca-Cola sign
that would redden and whiten like the eye of an insomniac.
The clock on the night-stand was like a face I could not reach.
A world widened in me. But what of my Protestant professors rearranging
furniture in their well-appointed heads,
hunched in their sepia-colored libraries?
Was it true, what they said, that a priest is a house lit up?

SPENCER REECE

At Swim Three Words

As my mother lay dying in a dark, cold room
where plumbing and ductwork were visible
overhead and cracks in cement walls sprouted
spider-webs and dust, I recalled the flume

that carried us pell-mell down, risible
in the extreme, at the Exhibition Grounds
in Vancouver, her mouth wide, kerchief
blown back, her body language quizzical,

as if laughter were verboten, out of bounds,
a thing unexpected, a joker outed
sans warning. When I stood by the bed,
my small hand clasped in hers, I had grounds

to wonder if she would die, though I doubted
this, of course, thinking only of myself,
my needs, days at the beach in English Bay
or Kitsilano, where I tossed sand, flouted

authority, sun-baked bodies, the air
reeking of seaweed, mustard, hot-dogs.
Some days I feel her speaking through me,
the few remaining strands of damp, brown hair

at sixes and sevens across her forehead,
lips pursed, facial muscles contracted
in a worry—ethics, clichés, beliefs,
each a clipped, forced whisper with its dread

finality. Resolute, I played the elf,
doing the dog-paddle across the frayed
linoleum, trying to make her laugh.
A tad of whimsy left on the back shelf

would suffice. She rallied briefly, half
alert, pulled herself into a sitting position,
the skin slack around her neck, eyes
closed from the effort. Grimace or laugh,

I know not, but she who swam kilometres
from Fisherman's Cove to Point Atkinson
managed a thin smile, patted my head
and traced on my body the necessary letters.

GARY GEDDES

Atocha 2004

The Caliph at Córdoba had a dizzying pool—
quicksilver from his mines at Almadén
sent glints and highlights wavering through the air
and set his guests and courtiers' heads to whirl.
It's ruined now—the palace's grand halls
unroofed and broken open to the sky.

On the all-night train from Lisbon to Madrid,
rumbling through the outskirts in the early dawn,
still gloomy, so the braziers flare bright
in trackside encampments and wrecking yards,
I think of commuters who check the time and yawn,
who'll be blown apart at the station up ahead.

There's a story that the bombs were to avenge
the last destruction of al-Andalus
which the Catholic Monarchs launched from Córdoba,
wresting Granada lovely from the Moors
five hundred years ago—itself revenge
for Arab conquest, eight hundred years before.

When they bombed Atocha we were safe at home
but preparing our first Spanish trip,
and our friends asked us if we'd 'cut and run'—
crude words which mimicked the Australian Right
still glorying in the capture of Baghdad.
But not to go would feel like giving in.

At Barcelona there's a mercury fountain:
quicksilver ripples out across the bowl,
in memory of the miners of Almadén
who rebelled from despair in '34,
who Franco, soon a rebel, came to crush.
This shimmering device revenges them.

Now we're at Atocha six months beyond the blast.
Angry tourists wave their tickets in the air,
urgent to board the fast train to Barcelona:
as if there's no call for the guard and his gun,
as if six months ago those travellers didn't die,
as if bombers didn't die their murderous death.

We've run to see Guernica, ate our paella,
rushed to send emails home to our kids,
eager—Catalonia and France lie ahead—
but surrounded by all Spain's silent dead.

DAVID BUNN

Breakfast at the Friar Arms

You say you'd like to move to St. Palendra
and kiss the stone we St. Palendrans kiss
on holy days on our elbows with a wick
burning in front of us at an altar. Well,
entering what looks like a badger hole
at the back of a fenced-off local cave,
you'd feel your rented helmet tapping
the underside of the Ralston Boulder,
named for one who preserved the site
by choking himself on strips of cloth
while his torturers were on ale break.
Once through, though, you'd relax.
Your eyes would adjust to a round
chamber banded with pink granite.
It'd be worth it, back at your hotel,
to say you'd received the blessing
as if it were your chance for fealty
to a toothless hag with a stone-axe
while a bearded furnace mechanic
conjured the names of fifty rebels
tethered to their ox-carts and hung
in pairs from trees along the roads
of St. Palendra—start and finish for
seditionists on their dirty hustings,
detested shire, blot on the imperial
shield, though nowadays promising
with our storm-watching weekends
and timeshare condos. What's that?
Your wife wants to tour the harbor?
Amble along the quay? I'll be here
if she should change her mind about
our discounted tour for barrow buffs
who contemplate a cottage on the bay.

PETER RICHARDSON

Children's Stories

The War was popular, with alluring cruelties:
at bedtimes, pressed, he might manage
some grim anecdote, small and
strangely lacking in heroics or apparent purpose:
the cold or some long dead soldier's rotten luck,
the terrible grinding of an engine
that promised death or
the Sten gun's many failings;
nothing any kid would ask for
and all of it given reluctantly.

But that head of his was full of stories
though we only got them later, told by
other mouths than his, mouths not stopped
in turn by reticence and earth:
the great sheds packed with tiny shoes,
the railheads and fences and him,
his weapons jammed and his tongue tied
while ghosts in legions, little groups, wagons
and rusty garments followed him down roads
and occupied the corridors he had to be in,
pleading in babels and when he woke
to smoke a sweat drenched cigarette,
lined by the bed, their fingers trembling,
reproaching him for lateness, for his failure
to fetch their children safely from the gates
of schools he couldn't name in streets he couldn't find,
in towns that tanks had ploughed away
and left to rot beneath the rain and failed harvests,
schools whose keys, in any case, were melted,
or crumbled in his fingers as they closed
around his nightly promises of rescue.

Meanwhile we dug garden camps, liberated Normandy,
fought hard at Arnhem, died over and again to overthrow Berlin
and made him join us in our victories, dragging at his sleeves
to make him come
until he sat and watched, fag on, tab end cupped for snipers
and commented on military technique
as you'd speak of something vain or sinful:
the forms of pride, perhaps,
or some vast gluttony.

PHILIP NUGENT

The Contortionist Speaks of Dislocation

The trick is not to care about connections. Then there's no pain
when ligaments twist and the shoulder pops from its socket,
when ribs accordion intercostals or heels bump
against the base of the skull and toenails scrape skin
from cheeks. The body is abandoned so clavicles can bend
backwards and the spine can arch to carry crown to coccyx.
Tendons forget and never know how to hold
their brother bones. Just a light nudge can push
their lax grip to anarchy. They slip away from woman
into an avalanche of buckled scaffolding, a game
of pick-up sticks, a car crumpled around the Pisa lean
of a streetlight, a cherry stem knotted in a closed mouth,
a crushed spider. The crowd cheers my collapse.

Once I was frozen. A shoebox under my bed holds
photos of a girl who tensed between the steel
of family on porch steps, stood stiff at the gate
of a Catholic school with books mooring her
to the cracked cement, and lay like a stone in the snow.
Each shutter snap clipped the same command
from the secret face behind it: capture a girl
beaten into hands without fidgets and irontight braids.
Nothing could be out of place. She is always out of place now.
Each night before muscles coax flesh to fold inwards
and cameras flash to catch this endless metamorphosis,
a square of memory is tucked away between the skin
and skintight suit. It lies below the left breast and counts
the heartbeats of each change. I need it there, I need it
after I let go, so the girl braced against picture clicks
can remind this body where the bones belong.

RACHEL LINDLEY

Delenda est Carthago

I too come from Carthage. I was there
as the city burned, as Scipio Africanus
came in from the sea—a bloody sunset,
a fiery night, six hundred years of city
sundered blood and rubble. Scipio
Africanus came in from the sea,
implacable with his legions, came in
from the sea implacable with his mission:
Carthage must be destroyed, must be
rendered void. Rome will have no rivals.
The ancient people, heirs of Tyre
and of Phoenicia, sold into slavery, those
that lived, or buried beneath the rubble.
A victory bloody and complete. I was there.

A victory bloody and complete. Carthage
must be destroyed. Citizens of Rome turned out
in force to cheer the murderous legions home.
A three day triumph through the city and Cato
vindicated. Carthage is no more. But Rome,
what of her, now master of the world?
The Senate in its celebration saw a future rich
with loot, its last rival gone. Instead it got
a hundred years of civil strife, of factions
fighting over African entrails. Assassinations,
riots and the death of the Republic.
I too come from Rome, I was there
in its martial glory and its slow civic
attrition born of triumph. I was there.

RON PRETTY

The Earth Moves and Bright

Hold on, the mother sings to herself
in the rain, holding her infant child
above the floodwaters. Hold on,
the orphan who sleeps standing up
will not let go of her doll. For one
hundred and one days they've been
waiting for the toxic waters to release
the souls of their loved ones. For one
hundred and one days they've been
praying for the children left behind.

We are a prehensile species, holding onto our children:
mothers giving birth in trees, remembering the lessons
of our simian ancestors, mothers holding on through
earthquake, hurricane and plague, when the earth
moves and bright angels, their bones bleached white,
the colour of mourning, fall through the cracks.

Now, after one hundred and one days,
the trees are receiving the voices of
souls come back. Does water polluted
by death without blessings, *le dernier*
priye, release the voices of angels or devils?
Who is it that speaks when the wind of
savage gods whispers in leaves watered
by innocent blood? Do not question the
mothers and children with the world in their
hands, just praise them for holding on.

Linda Rogers

Earthquake Light

March 11, 2011

Earlier tonight an owl nailed the insomniac white hen.
She'd fluttered up onto a fence post to peer at the moonlight,
to meditate in her usual way on the sadness of the world

and perhaps the hundreds of vanished eggs of her long life here.
I was watching from the porch and thinking she ought not to be
where she was, and then she wasn't, but taken up, a white hankie

diminishing in the east, one the owl would not ever drop.
Now an hour after, the new night wind spins up a leghorn ghost
of her fallen feathers under the moon and along the meadow grass:

corpse candle, friar's lantern, will-o'-the-wisp chicken soul
dragging its way toward me, that I might acknowledge her loss
and her generosity, and wonder again about her longstanding

inability to sleep on certain nights. There are sky lights
beyond our understanding and dogs whose work it is to scent
the cancer no instrument can see. On the nights she could not sleep,

the hen Cassandra Blue perched herself with clear view to the east
and studied the sky, every two seconds canting her head a few degrees
one way or the other. What she saw or if she saw it I cannot say,

though it seemed that something always somewhere was about to go
badly wrong. Then again, it always is. Now there's a swirl
of wind in the meadow, spinning three or four final white feathers

west to east across it, and there's a coyote come foolishly out
into the open, hypnotized by feather flicker, or scent, then seeing
by moonlight the too-blue shimmer of my eyes, and running for its life.

ROBERT WRIGLEY

An Embarrassment of Riches

I

Our first full day in Zambia, a family in an old oil-burning Beetle called
to welcome us to town. While the grown-ups talked, I opened crates

and boxes: found a pile of Marvel Comics, scale model die-cast toys,
the Field Commander Action Man with life-like hair and gripping hands

I'd got for Christmas. The shoeless, wide-eyed neighbour boys stared
openly, stood mesmerized, as if suddenly exposed to works of alien

pornography, or posing in an amateur tableau evoking Sodom, Lot's
defiant wife. My new friends left with borrowed Beanos, dog-eared

Famous Five adventure books, a stack of Captain Britain weeklies—
said they'd pay me back. That night I slept uncovered, left the light

on in the hall—awoke to a cacophony of crickets, croaking frogs.
In the shadows, tailless geckos moved sure-footed on the walls.

II

Food shortages were commonplace. Rhodesia cut off milk and meat,
blocked the open trade of cocoa beans, preserves and packaged sweets.

Cars were much the same—my father searched for weeks to find an old
estate, bought a third-hand Morris Minor crank start off of Jimmy Crabb,

a Scotsman fond of crimplene, garish stay-prest slacks—short-sleeved
shirts and belted jackets in the style of early African explorers. Along

with outsized hedgehog flies and bees came painted locusts, mixed
varieties of lizard, praying mantids, raids of army ants—our garden

was a lush and unspoiled paradise of sub-Saharan fauna flanked on every
side by cyclone fencing topped with razor wire. A neighbour told my father

that the local Bemba children often shimmied underneath to steal ripe fruit—
claimed he kept a rifle in the kitchen, said it put the wind up thieving munts.

III

The motionless agamas found on rooftops, wide-trunked mango trees
and flowering acacias often plagued me in my dreams, freed fight-or-flight

anxieties, released inchoate feelings of aversion, fear, hostility. Blue-throated
alpha-males would bob their heads aggressively, engage in combat—use

their armour-piercing tails as deadly weapons. When chased they reached
alarming speeds. The one I chance-encountered after running to retrieve

an errant cricket ball was monstrous—hissed like a corn snake, made
my muscles seize. Though charmed, I kept my wits and backed up slowly,

called for the garden boy in Bantu—found him underneath the shade trees
rubbing wax on our estate. Once murdered the agama lost its colour, left no

ornament to decorate its death—just lay there flattened in the dust. We left
it belly up, went in—ate pickled beets and tinned ham sandwiches for lunch.

PHILLIP CRYMBLE

Four Trees

As you narrow your eyes and focus
I follow the line of your sight
to the prospect of order before us:

four trees in equipoise. The thrust
of it—symmetrical, plumb—excites
you. I narrow my eyes and focus

on colour, nonplussed
by this arboreal (your favourite)
prospect of order. Before us

were water-lilies—all blooming fuss
and clutter—but right
now you'd rather all eyes refocused

on this long-extinct border—this locus
amoenus, you call it (lost overnight
on a prospector's orders). Before us,

I say, the proof of disorder—life on the cusp
of loss. You save that fight
for later, and narrow your eyes. You focus:
the prospect of order before us.

DONALD GIVANS

The Garbage Truck Trashed the Sunflower

It had just overtaken the fence, springing
colour over the grey-flecked cedar boards
that enclosed the small garden and yard.

I imagine its big head hit with a thwunk
on the lane of compacted gravel and dirt.
Of course, nobody heard it, and the chances

are nobody saw what were the pincer-like
hydraulic arms side-swiping the tall stalk
during the dust-up of high-pitched stops

and starts forking from bin to bin. I don't
blame the driver—there isn't much time
to collect all that garbage. What's the life

of one sunflower? Sure, I planted it there
and it grew heavy-headed until it leaned out
into the lane a little, but I didn't want to tie it

to the fence. Besides, a magnum opus of sun-
flower centres the yard like the tuba's high
note blasting the brightest yellow of the year.

Its six-foot stalk stands straight against gravity,
but its hunched neck bends as if it'll break
under the weight of its seedless head peering

onto sweet peas, salad blooms and the carrot
leaves that dance in the gentle breeze. For some
time now, carbon has questioned many things

green. Though the end is certain, the sun will
only shine through the spindles of red maple
that way this time. The fractured light will stay

on the gold band of petals like fire licks only
so long. If I look long enough, I feel happy,
even laugh. And the light has changed already.

JEFF STEUDEL

The Grasshoppers' Silence

Listen to the story the prisoner's wife
hears in the Bengali darkness: the
one he'd told her about a grasshopper
he'd caught in his sweep net at dusk
and taken home in a glass jar with
breathing holes punched in the lid.

"Why do boys catch insects?" she'd asked,
and he'd answered: *"Because they are lonely."*

He told her the alarmed grasshopper
fiddled, rubbing its leg against its
belly. In Bangladesh, as in China,
ancient violins have one string; and
they sing in minor keys. "Why is their
music so sad?" she asked him, even
though she already knew the answer.

"Their music is sad because grasshoppers are sad."

In Bangladesh, unfaithful women are
called "grasshoppers," because the
adulteresses jump from leaf to leaf
in monsoon swamps. "Don't ever leave
me," her husband had ordered his
captive insect, pulling off one of its
legs before he made it a suit of rags.

"Did it ever sing after that?" she'd asked.

His wife was a curious woman who'd
gazed past the Chittagong Hills to praise
the sunrise, its clamorous golds and

vermilions. "Don't you ever leave me,"
he'd said to her every time she opened
a book or looked out the window, her
eyes astonished as water lilies opening
to the first light of dawn. And that one
last time, "You left me," tearing out her
eyes and leaving them both alone in the
dark—her in a room without windows and
him in the prison he'd made for himself,
listening to the grasshoppers' silence.

LINDA ROGERS

The Infinite Library

There's a man climbing the book stacks, all he's read
behind and beneath him, part now of the firmament
on which he balances his ladder. He has been a long time
climbing, reading as he goes. He remembers it all,
no need to down-climb, backtrack, reread. Long
as his years of climbing, his recollection of all he's read,
hands, eyes and feet all fluency, economy; deft and steady
his ascent. He keeps to hard-bound literature. Anthologies
and well-read authors make the soundest steps. From time
to time he stumbles upon a slim volume of obscure origin,
whose weight belies the name. These he carries with him,
letting go only when the burden of whispers
buckles his legs, sending a tremor through the edifice.
Like feathers they drift into darkness, no echo returning
to tell of the fall. Even as he climbs, reads, climbs,
the stacks grow taller, yet he never tires, each shelf
firing his attempt at the next. No lack of oxygen
in the bookish air and ever the chance of a fresh breath,
something not quite new but sharp enough to raise a gasp,
release a sigh. Quiet as a dust mote circulating in a light shaft
between the towering stacks he climbs, directed
by the voice of every author, accompanied by every
character. All his life, it seems, he has been climbing,
paragraph by paragraph, page upon page, book stacks
growing ahead and behind. Never enough time, never
enough light for so much yet unread. Still he climbs,
having come so far, unsure now of the way down,
knowing how deep the silence that greets the fall.

Jillian Pattinson

The Kingfisher

For Maureen Harris

And so each bird throws the idea of herself
      ahead of herself, up the river—
A line of spiritual thought without a sinker—
And flies after it. As if the actual could ever hope to reel the ideal in. But so it is
That awareness of the azure kingfisher—a dark electricity, a plump
Trim elegance of intent—reaches you on the riverbank
      that last warm Sunday of autumn, split seconds

Before the bird; so that when she passes you at light speed, her name
      is already a bright blue phrase on your tongue, is already
      the unresolved cadence of your second self.

MARK TREDINNICK

Late Breaking News

We're in Wally's Renault, driving
south in Provence, the car radio
harvesting disaster, swaths of it,

and the fields bloody with tulips,
a brash statement stretching
to the low hills of the Luberon.

Later, in the hilltop fortress
with its catapult and trebuchet,
I ask my friend what happened

to monks, to sanctuary, places
where little pain sears the weary
breastbone, where envy's rare

as gourmet meals, where even
the spirited horse, grown
accustomed to lassitude, nudges

the pitchfork's worn handle until
hay falls like manna from the loft,
and where prayers are crafted

in lieu of weapons. Eternity
is long, Pascal has written, so
faith is worth the gamble.

The soul sets sail for a distant
port. Tears mark its departure,
but what marks its arrival?

Planks resound with footsteps,
deep water parts to accommodate
the insistent keel. Wally, amused,

dismisses these speculations,
insists there's romance
in neither monastery nor rose.

Solace, perhaps, though skimpy,
and only in what the moving pen
inscribes or the stiff horse-hairs

of the brush render permanent
and lovely, those moments, all
too brief, when the anchor holds

and the sea blooms resplendent
with all manner of kelp and with the
scrubbed tulip faces of the dead.

GARY GEDDES

Leaving the Island

We've all gone now, left the place to the sheep
and the gannet, the puffin and the wren.

For decades only a mailboat of whalebone and oak
came and went from here. Then the tourists

arrived to see if we were more than myth in the Outer
Hebrides. We sold them tweed and spotted

bird's eggs, let them look in on prayer meetings, count
the stones in the walls we built to keep out the weather.

When we prayed it was for a cease
to things: the wind, the war, the plagues.

In the end, the land choked us out, carcasses
of sea birds and layers of peat moss turned to lead

the constant fog, the solitude, the slippery grass
by the cliff's edge, that impossible winter of 1929.

We left our Bibles open and handfuls of oats on the floor.
Locked our doors behind us. From this vantage point

our home was just a sketch of land that shrank into the sea—
the island's sharp crags impossible to understand.

This land, so angry and so peaceful now, without
us. The feral sheep bleat into the evening.

Nothing to bother them but old age and the wind
that made us all walk like bent trees.

TALYA RUBIN

Leopold

It's alright Leopold you can relax now
There's no need to plan another tour
Everyone can see you weren't exaggerating
Everyone agrees your son's a star
And you don't need leave from Salzburg anymore
With the Prince-Archbishop gone from power

With Colloredo gone (relax) your son's the power
Who's taken all before him so that now
Your surname's not your surname anymore
(More ways than you could advertise on tour
Watching and hearing the child star)
But a byword for music and mastery past exaggerating

For beauty and genius past hope of exaggerating
The whole world knows his power
And follows the Mozart star
Even to praise or blame his father now
(Don't laugh) for attitudes or incidents or risks on tour
To royal houses that don't matter anymore

Leopold it doesn't matter anymore
What anyone or Wolfgang tries exaggerating
In home town service and on European tour
You've done your best with your employer and every other power
So prodigies and parents then till now
Can hate or hail you as a guiding star

From your first joy in your infant star
(The play of fear) till after you couldn't teach him anymore
As child or adolescent or as adult now
With warning and advising and exaggerating
Dangers of travel and marriage and power
By letter when you couldn't be on tour

Like when your wife instead of you on tour
Died past planning in Paris leaving the young star
All alone and all grown up to power
Leopold you just can't do this anymore
With the Prince-Archbishop dead and no exaggerating
You and your son more than two centuries dead now

Leopold the tour is over you can rest now
With all your family with the star raised to a higher power
Needing no strategies for exaggerating anymore

David Mortimer

Lise Meitner Leaves Berlin

Born into a Viennese Jewish family, physicist Lise Meitner helped
to discover nuclear fission in Germany before fleeing the country
in 1938.

I'm taking off my lab coat
for the last time.
Each piece of apparatus stands in place:
cloud chamber, electrometer,
a web of wires to trap lightning.

Today I'm saying goodbye
to Frau Professor,
the Jewess with the worthless brain.
Tomorrow I'll leave my flat
with nothing but a jacket,
an address in Holland
I might never find.

For too long, Otto, I've worn the white
of this sanctuary for science,
possessed, like you, by the prize,
my head filled with atoms.
Do we know, even now,
what demons' eyes we've lit?

One neutron and a chain reaction,
one word to turn a crowd
and shatter the world.

When I could take the tram home
I'd see young women in the Tiergarten
pushing prams,
boys chasing round trees

waving wooden guns,
girls with ropes,
men reading newspapers.
Even then I could guess the headlines.

They say Vienna waltzed after the Anschluss.
Everywhere people are dancing
to the music of broken glass.

I'm saying good night, Otto.

My lab coat hangs lifeless
behind the door,
notes on my workbench
a muddled epitaph,
the electrometer's needle
back to zero.

Victor Tapner

Morel-Floored Forest

Like as the hart desireth the water-brooks
so longeth my soul after thee . . .
  —Psalm 42 *Coverdale Bible*

O
mushrooms
so epicurean,
as knights their grail,
shepherdesses their lambs,
thus I
search
for you
morels,
grown up
below oak—
fungi that jut from leaf-mulch
ground that fosters musty birth
of such saintly/earthy fleshpots

O
the paroxysms
of my disbelief greet
fist-fat conical hats (on
cream-bottomed stems) which
strive to achieve tower height
such that
my basket
husbands
black masses—
gargantuan drowsers to be plucked
from their beds: the mushroom sheep
take up plump and bulbous positions

Morels along the paths of forest floor, when one kneels to them, always be-
stow an annunciation (sometimes seconded by sunbeam, dappled through
tree-crown) upon the seeker of their lift-of-sorrow essence/their lichen-
sprung luscious pungency/their undeniably desirable spongy glory.

CAROLYN HOOPLE CREED

Mosaic

This is how you kiss me,
hard, your hand on my throat.
Your tongue slides along my teeth.
It feels like the wing
of a small bird on my lips.
Your mouth moves over my skin,
and like a magnet
brings to the surface
the parts of me that are real.
My body in fragments, the pieces of me wet.
You put me back together,
a mosaic you design from my remains.

This is my offering.
I kneel before you, no longer broken.
Your body, the curve of your arm,
the tightness of your thigh,
is the altar where I learn to pray.
Take it, you say. All of me.
I take the part of you
that is unforgiving and hard,
the part of you that carries
the secrets and dreams
of the women you have loved.

I feel your chest rise and fall,
at first slowly, then fast and deep.
You become still,
the way lake water calms
before a windstorm.
My voice breaks, Come, I whisper.
I am baptized, a sinner cleansed in holy water.
You are the wafer on my tongue.

You taste like warm rain and salt,
something the spirits created
to tempt me and keep me thirsty.
I find redemption in the way
the taste of you lingers,
and in the outline of your mouth
when you smile.

Polyxeni Angelis

The Need for These Things to Be Said

For Donald Woods

The baby grand, its mouth gaping, is robbed of children's practice books.
The police retreat with pens, pencils, and sheet music.
Donald Woods, leaning his elbow beside the keys,
faces the one-way night window.
Wendy, his wife, stands away from the glass, mimes
the daily inquest proceedings—fingers, leg irons, fists, police trucks.
Donald wipes a finger under his glasses,
nods.

For this editor, the Restricted Persons Act tapes his mouth shut,
fuses this writer's fingers with law.
Upstairs, his children fall into sleep, his wife reads.
Across the keyboard, from a childhood Christmas, his uncle
draws on a postcard the three movements of a sonata.
Woods stalls at the keys, a writer with no pens learning
Chopin with no books.

The bullet that entered the living room window last night, that hush
bullet wrapped in the scowl of the neighbours,
made a hole the size of a rand.
Now the wind-filled smells of cooking come in, and go out, in breaths
—a strange asset for the house-bound—a glass tracheotomy.
Donald loosens his tie, heels to the ground,
right foot brushing the sustain pedal.
He centers himself on the stool, back to the window
while they dare not shoot him.

Ninhydrin!
For lifting prints at crime scenes is lifting the skin from his five year old.
His child is sedated, but he is awake.
Writing is lifting ninhydrin from his hands and pressing the keys violet. He types:

"No fear can outweigh the need for these things to be said."
The poisoned t-shirt is in the bag, but
not the one they're packing.

At New Year, the watchers go on the nod, the piano falls silent.
For this escape, each word is learned by heart.
The music has been called up and stored—
a deep breath for an underwater swim. A cassock, the editor's mantle.
Fireworks spark from the watchtower into the night and fizz.
The international audience sits, legs politely crossed at the ankles, waiting for
Woods to play freely
for Biko

Margaret McCarthy

Night Thoughts from Somewhere Past High Noon

Roadwork everywhere, jackhammers nattering on
 like mosquitos escaped from a drive-in schlockflick.
Call it a day the late sun says but then lingers
 lightly on the western porch like some bright-eyed guest
reluctant to depart and you can see why, having
 been all day struck by its riveting midsummer
rise, the light insistent on its own absolute
 rectitude, poised for hours against that slow plunge
towards the smoulder of old midwinter moonshine—
 that the sky god will rise again—as yes it will,
unlike me, say, whose turn comes only once,
 no matter what our phallic fables might pretend.
I solve the sphinx's riddle merely by living
 the answer, hoping to carve my initials *scritch-*
scratch-scritch in the thick-skinned world I happen through,
 thinking hell they'll last like eximious dinosaur
shit, but knowing the numbers tell a different tale.
 Midsummer's where I am and lingering on the porch—
 downhill from here, the easiest leg, though hardest
 on the knees; their bent gets awkwarder all the time,
but nothing that good shoes, aspirin, and surgery
 can't delay till Hamlet in hiking boots mutates
into this slow-mo Lear doing Tai Chi barefoot
 on the heath beside that nipped and tucked and still (thanks
to pharmaco-chemistry) well fucked Tony and Cleo.
 You go gently guys! the heckler in my brain yells,
teenaged even now, addled with its own juice.
 I love my life like sunlight, oysters, and the dulled
pain of dental surgery, but know that the fat
 hump of irony which adorns my hairless back
will not keep the coffin lid from closing down, down,
 or stop the hearse's jaunt the way roadwork just might.

IAIN HIGGINS

The Old Man and the Beanstalk

Three beans in the clay pot,
one for each hope left to the old man.
A week passes with soil still bare,
watered by thick hands,
until the morning a single stalk
bends its neck to the sun.

Noon. He waits for his son,
beef stew cooking in the pot,
rises, once, to check the slight, green stalk.
The night smells of burnt onion. The man
does not eat and the door handle
does not turn, too shy to bear

his steadfast gaze and bare
itself in turn. The morning sun
unrolls its slow heat a handsbreath
across the sill, limns the clay pot
and the table where the old man
sleeps, restless. The beanstalk

seems no bigger, lacks more stalks
for context. Dream bares
its throat to waking. The man
finds a brief message from his son,
who is sorry he forgot. A pot
of coffee later, the shaking in his hands

has faded. He soaks the soil in handfuls
of water, tender of the brown stalk.
He is sorry he let the pot
dry. A story then, low-voiced, of a bare
field that grew a sturdy beanstalk and a son
who climbed it and became a man,

or maybe a thief. Where is a man
who can reach that high, hands
giving instead of taking? Too much sun—
the old man is baked as dry as the stalk.
He spills out two dead beans, the stalk and the barren
earth, then walks away from the empty pot.

ALINA WILSON

Old Men on a Bench

Of the ability we still have of walking on slippery ground
to where the boats are moored; of levitating,
not in cultivated gardens but, against all advice,
on the fishing dock itself, its smells more uplifting than yoga;
of imagining our children helpless in foreign cities—
our excuse, through subterfuges of anger, to ruffle
travel agents, hurry the issuing of visas—we speak,
carefully, pressing another's hands should the need arise,
counselling patience, as though drawing up plans
for a new building we're certain, one day, to share.

Our words may seem to you, eavesdropper, to skip over surfaces,
like today's last dragonfly before it's absorbed by shadow,
and some things may be clearer to you later,
much later, like, as every evening darkened, we imagined
we'd lift off the bench without effort
and sail home as steady as herons.

ADIL JUSSAWALLA

On Finding a Copy of "Pigeon" in the Hospital Bookstore

I prowled up and down the rows of the hospital bookstore with a fevered intensity;
"fevered" because it was a hospital, "intensity" because I was perplexed by
the mysteriously ruptured tendon in the middle finger of my right hand
in sympathy with which the whole hand had cramped
so that I could scarcely hold a pen or open a jar.
Even a five-month-old octopus in the Munich zoo can open a jar!

The octopus's name is Frieda, which reminded me
of D.H. Lawrence, and thinking of him
brought me to the hospital bookstore. It was minimally stocked
with anything resembling literature, offering those in pain,
afraid, or just dully waiting for test results
a choice of pink-jacketed chick-lit, cookbooks, investment guides
or glossy thrillers spilling blood
as red as that pooling down the hall in the O.R.,
as though emulating some homeopathic principle
of curing a disease by a surfeit of that which caused it.

And perched as eccentrically as the sparrow who sings from the rafters
at Loblaws, and looking just as lost,
was the only volume of poetry in the store.
Reading it I recognized at once what I disliked
about the bulky bestsellers nudging it from the shelf
like bullies in the halls of high school, their meaty faces
full of self-regard, their minds absent of thought.
I hate the omni-present present tense, that fake cinematic contrivance
meant to create a sense of "being in the moment" with the hero
as though life were a constant rush of adrenaline
with no possible mood but surprise.

Whereas poetry offers the results of its meditation
tentatively; it is not embarrassed to show that thinking
—some of it slow, arduous, confused—has taken place.
And then poetry doesn't rush ahead shouting, "Look at me! Look at me!"
Instead, it takes your hand, your poor mangled hand, like the good surgeon it is
and massages it joint by joint, feeling for the sore places.
And because it doesn't speak without reflection
you trust it, and let it cut you open.

SUSAN GLICKMAN

Paradiso

In a garden they had named their Paradiso
The garage stands with the door always ajar
An old man in the evening waters roses
Plastic flowers grow amid some Pampas grass.

In a garden—and its name is Paradiso
an old woman sets the table for some tea
A veil of lilac blue perfume dances around her
for an instant she's become his young new wife.

In this garden—and its name is Paradiso
Flags of laundry fly their colours in the wind
A picnic table, plastic chairs, mismatched companions
the man whistles for the stray cats to come back.

There's a garden whose name is Paradiso
An old barbecue leans rusting by the vine
Smells of rhubarb, dandelions and wild garlic
Water barrels stand forgotten in the rain.

In the garden whose name is Paradiso
she finds solace as she sits there in the shade
she remembers the good times when they gathered for a feast
Sunday afternoons with friends long gone away.

In her dreams she named this garden Paradiso
In wrought iron its name written on the gate
It doesn't matter—just a dream—the garden lives still within
And she loves him among the stray cats and the rain.

In this garden whose name is Paradiso
There's a teapot on the table, and two cups.
So I miss you but you don't know that you're not here.
We have tea in conversation with stray cats.

MARIA BORYS

The Pardon

Tyburn Gallows, 1447

Slavish to the letter of the law or perhaps just plain
    Malefic, the hangman refuses to return his due
        And the gallowbirds—babe-naked, marked for

Quartering from Adam's apple to navel—scarcely
    Dare meet each other's eye as the messenger
        Spurs his nag back to town. Should they kick

Up a fuss? Demand their earthly goods, wood-soled
    Shoes and shirts, the woolen hose holding each
        Wearer's shape like a ghost? Thwarted, the mob

Rumbles, a faint thunder on the horizon…one felon
    Takes his cue and strides off, rubbing at the roadmap
        Inked upon his chest with an idle thumb. One sits

Poleaxed at the platform's edge; the Wheel has spun
    Too fast to catch his breath. Laughing madly, two leap
        Down to join their drunken friends while the last

Looks blinking around him, shaken awake to this
    Shadow-dream—the rain-dark fields, glinting leaves,
        Kingfisher and reeds of a high summer day—then

Stiffly, like an old man, begins his journey back.

ELLEN WEHLE

The Silence

The dead we know are gone except
when dreams return them. So it was
Frank Sargeson took me aside

in Hell and said, 'You know, my friend,
how well the wind among the reeds
is used by shaman and guru,

rabbi and priest.' He had the face
of Dante's much-loved preceptor
Brunetto Latini among

the sodomites, as we ambled
down the avenues of the damned;
and he, brushing ash from his sleeve

went on, 'Those with a patch of earth
and running water lack vision,
preferring to leave such mysteries

'to desert- and mountain-dwellers
and the poor of Varanasi.
Where little is lacking listen

'always to the silence until
you hear it whisper its name.' So
he faded into fire, and I,

half-waking, wrote to remember
all that he'd said—and listened for
the silence, and could not hear it.

C.K. STEAD

Spring in Cow Bay, Nova Scotia

After A.F. Moritz

Sad coasts that even these weeks of unrelenting rain
from clouds assuming squatters' rights cannot make
sadder. They drench silver picnic sands long denuded,
scraped to build docks for container ships, landing strips
for naval aircraft to muster local jobs, beach rendered
defenseless in Atlantic hurricanes; the coast receding
ever further, nothing to look at. For whoever has not
from him shall be taken away even that he has. The old
family cemetery is held in check between commuters'
new-builts where tides and ties exert their pull, and surf's
adventuring gliders on their circuit. Abraded stones
soft among rain-green patches blanketing unknowns
and long-forgottens, the swollen yard's one small scar
takes the rain as though to nourish new ashes, this
closing-out-of-sequence, youngest sister. Our practice
of containment. We too as wraiths—unrecognizable,
scraped-away grains inhabiting new ports and runways, receding
ever further, coasts of mind removed to another place.

BARBARA MYERS

The Stiltwalkers

We arrived on horseback. Villagers pooled
around us, faces kind & open. We drugged the water.
We constructed their poverty from scratch.
Poured wine on each other's heads, laughing,
dubbing ourselves kings. Introduced a new law:
each foot of each villager would be severed
& upon each stump a tall wooden stilt be sewn,
so they could not escape the woods. They turned
on us. My comrades fled. I heard the stilts on
cobblestones at midnight like a thunder.
I escaped my palace to the brink of a deep barranca
singing my death chant & hurled myself in.
I survived. Now I walk among them, disguised
as an old woman, feet strapped to stilts,
ankles blistered, toes smashed. They eye me
at market, but I do not break. I hobble to my room
under the stairs. Peel off the mask & wool dress.
O, freedom becomes them. They have grown eloquent
in walking. Running faster than we ever could.
Tall as birches. Their young born that way:
attached. I hear their voices, drowning phonemes,
through the floors. I do not make a sound.
I am afraid to look, but each night I peek out
at their street dances. They lope like puppets &
never fall. Women gyrate in a ring around the bonfire.
Behind, the men jump, ever higher, calling for love.
Women catch them. Everyone begins to spin,
these giants, arms upraised, slowly, then blurring—
impossibly—& sing in a collective low
moan the joy of their dark hearts like gods.

JOHN WALL BARGER

Sun Flower Sutra

Was this, indeed, what it was supposed to be like,
New York, in summer, this sumac-leaved stammer,
the landscape of ineradicable grit, and towers built
as though to escape the ground they bedded in?

She walked south on Canal past City Hall choked
with an ingress of the smallest cogs of governance.
It was 8:43, and the morning light felt like coarse
linen on the fine lines of her face, her arms exposed.

A dog was peeing, a gusher washing dust from
a front tire, an Escalade's, braced against the curb.
Now, the water came up to lap at its rocky bank.
A derelict tried for a quarter and shambled away.

"And what street compares with Mott Street," she
thought, and thought of Nathan Road where she'd
bought red silk panties whose color bled, staining
the inside of her thighs the first time she wore them.

Somehow, the signs had become confused. One
whispered "79th" and another "3rd Ave." A kiosk
guarded the corner. Doughy pretzels hung looped
from a wooden cart, its owner off taking a leak.

Then, the city turned over, its concrete radiating
heat into the suffocating air. The sky fell open.
A bloom like a dust of pollen overlay the dead cars.
She became the ash the sun scattered everywhere.

STUART JAY SILVERMAN

Tamarind Tree

There are just two people left who can speak [Ayapaneco] . . .
but they refuse to talk to each other. –The Guardian

Talk to me beneath the tamarind tree. Before it's too late,
let us bury our quarrel in Tabasco's lowlands. I am old and my heart stutters.
Let us talk beneath the feathery foliage and wide pinnate leaves.
Only we remember the hum and click of our grandmothers' tongues.

Let us bury our quarrel in Tabasco's lowlands. We are old and our hearts stutter.
Why do you avoid me on the street, at the market, in the Zocalo?
Only we remember the hum and click of our grandmothers' tongues.
Before our blood runs dry, speak to me of kolo-golo-nay

on the street, at the market, in the Zocalo. Why do you avoid me?
Rest on this bench awhile. Above us pods bulge white flesh.
Before our blood runs dry, speak to me of kolo-golo-nay
and skins that grow brittle, pulp that turns to a sticky paste.

The pods above us bulge white flesh. Rest on this bench awhile.
Or shake the drooping branches and watch the fruit fall.
The skins grow brittle; the pulp turns to a sticky paste.
Last week another anthropologist washed up on our linguistic island.

She shook the drooping branches just to watch the fruit fall.
What lies between us but three sleeping dogs and a litter of cracked shells?
Another anthropologist has washed up on our linguistic island.
O to be reborn, a flat brown bean along a tree's young shoot.

Lying between us: three sleeping dogs, a litter of cracked shells.
Brother, we speak two different versions of the same stubborn truth.
O to be reborn, a flat brown bean along a tree's young shoot,
but the rain falling on Ayapa sounds a death knell clatter.

Two different versions of the same stubborn truth? Speak to me, brother,
beneath the feathery foliage and wide pinnate leaves.
Listen: the rain falling on Ayapa sounds a death knell clatter.
Before it's too late, talk to me beneath the tamarind tree.

PATRICIA YOUNG

Themba is Dead

Themba is dead
He lies in a coffin of wood
Garment of cotton
Stockings of wool
stiff as stone

Themba is dead
Taking his grief to grave
Hoping never again to be black

Themba is dead
Fifteen years ago
when he crossed the sea alive ·
Hopes decorated with fantasies of a white life
He lived in the shadows of others
No chance in the light
He struggled in the dark

Themba is a fool
wise only yesterday
Today he is in a coffin of wood
Garment of cotton
Stockings of wool
Stiff as stone

Now...

The municipality is taking samples
consulting the law
Making phone calls
checking cost
To decide which land owns Themba

EMEKA OKEREKE

There You Are

Even once aboard, I feel the stinging cold
and as the train begins to heave

away from the old country station,
away from the spiny, alabaster mountains,

I see you,
crossing your arms in midair,

again and again,
your face alit.

At my seat, I prepare to collapse;
in my head I am already in the city.

Ten hours into the future, I sink into my bed,
next to the woman waiting in it,
and tell her of your joyous farewell.

Now, I drop my bags and watch you through the window.

You recede in slowest motion,
your eyes singing,

your whole-bodied smile gently mocking
my exhaustion.

The morning is illumined by your gesture,
not by the stingy sun.

The scarf wrapped round your head
sounds a note of vivid colour,
defying the gravelly sky.

For the last time, you wave your arms,
and I make a noise like a laugh,
astonished by the contrast between us:

you are so young,
I am so old.

Not ten years afterward I dip a shovel
into a mound of earth,
and hear the dirt smack dryly on polished wood,

and begin to describe you
to different women, in different cities.

There's the train, there's the distance;
no more station, no more mountains.

There you are,
slowly windmilling your arms,
                              and smiling.

MITCHELL ALBERT

They Disappeared in the Night

They disappeared in the night as the white ash of
the fire went cold. They disappeared with the tales
the almond tree had overheard. Only the stray
mountain goat and the restless stones that
wandered with our people for years knew their
story.

You must understand they left us the way a leper
leaves you living in the weak house of your skin.
It was late in the life of spring how could this
happen?

We searched for signs; a feather from a striped
bird, or the fruit of the peach tree wearing the skin
of the elders. Who would lead us now? The voice
of reason was dead and still dying as we argued
into the next day.

Then the old woman spoke: A nightingale is only a
nightingale when it confesses its brightest colours
are hidden in its throat and a dog becomes the
animal we know when it pulls love out of the cruel
master's hand.

And as the mangled tree straightened a branch our
tongues curled and no one spoke. And the silence
fell, and it fell like a man falling off a cliff without
having one moment to shout out his name, only the
silence filling his body, then the gorge, then the
lives of all who knew him. This was the traveling
silence, the twin of sorrow that knocks on every
door and never tires.

RAFI AARON

Three Monkeys on a Dusty Bureau

On his dusty bureau,
beside the mint lifesavers
my grandfather had a carving of three dark monkeys.
See no evil, hear no evil, speak no evil.
"Which one are you?" he would ask.
"I don't have enough hands to decide," I replied.
"Eventually, everyone must choose," he said dropping
another ice cube into his drink.

I left home without ever knowing which he had settled on.
My astute arrogance buffered by courageous ignorance,
convinced my life would be free of such passive despair.
I would never face the same decisions.

Now as I settle into this age of glorious imperfections
with its wrinkles and various indignities,
before the promised wisdom had settled upon these tired shoulders,
and the fierceness of youth is whittled down into memory as thin as hair,
I wait in the mornings with my neighbours
at the train station.
Their faces clutched in concentration,
lips filled with woes they don't consider petty.
An unfocussed restlessness
disturbs the finely ordered
rhythm of my day.

More than ever I need the tenderness of understanding.
Now, I wish those monkeys rested on my bureau.
But they are gone.
Sold in some anonymous yard sale.
And still, I have not chosen.

SHELAGH MCNALLY

Tsunami

Grief comes in waves.
I didn't see you coming.
I'd kept guard for three years
then packed away the sandbags.

My desert island,
so far from the epicenter of you,
I didn't think you'd ever
shake me again.

Your shifting
should have gone unnoticed,
your movements
unannounced,

never again to ripple
my safe harbour.
But the news crashed
through me

like a tsunami,
tore up my shallow roots,
shredded the new growth,
left me like driftwood.

Grief comes in waves,
hits without warning.
You can't fight the ocean,
only try not to drown.

So I will lie here
till my sodden splinters dry
and the sand beneath me is solid.
Even now, I can feel the tsunami receding,

trickling back
to the rocks tears puddle under,
to hide in the hollows of me,
seeping away in streams

to wherever grief goes,
to be still,
lap quietly,
and wait.

BRONWYN LOVELL

Unlimited

it's a monolith, thought the gull
alighting on her shoulder

a monument, mused the spirit
whistling through her walls

a pillar, whispered the wind
twirling 'round her limbs

a village, revealed the crier
surveying her space

a forest, roared the storm
swirling about her hair

a poem, sang the song
hearing a lute in her hum

a damask, decided the novel
etching a tale on her skin

with the sky in one eye
and the ocean in the other

she decides she's
the gut of the earth

SUPARNA GHOSH

Walking Underwater

For Kim Stafford

There is this quietness that hangs over North America.
As if all the days were double-glazed against themselves.
It's uncanny. Tectonic. A kind of grief, a kind of pain
In waiting. Some sort of business unfinished. I feel it here
In the northwest, especially, though it stalked me in Toronto:
A slender quality of northern light, I guess, my southern
Self's unused to, transposed into a season of suppressed sound,
A penumbra of silence cast by too much history, too much
Ecstatic landscape, too many plot points resolved at gunpoint,
And it feels like my life's been lost here from the start.

I'm sorry: I'm talking out of my mood, which is jet-lagged
And dreaming heavily of what it used to think I loved.
There are plates subducting other plates on the mantle
Of my mind; there is disquiet and illness of ease. But look,
Out your windows the prayer flags have stopped
Praying, and moss deckles the edges of the oaks and firs,
Which hold out stoically inside the sweetest excuse for day-
Light I've ever seen. Come out with me, you say; let's wander
Up the river. Let's see what N'chi wana has to say about
The light… Which turns out to be a lot, and most of it profane—

The cock and the cunt, for instance, Neruda's entanglement
Of genitals, right there, gargantuan in basalt, and wrapped in Douglas
Fir on the south bank—and glorious. The robins along the Eagle
Creek drainage seemed convinced it was spring, but the cloud
That streamed downriver on the back of the teal-blue water
And the rising wind and the narrow road coming unstuck beneath
Our feet, were all busy putting winter back in place. And for two
Hours you schooled me in the art of walking underwater; for two
Hours we carried a bright conversation all the way to the falls
And back again in rain that fell like disappointment on my head.

If you're going to call a mountain range The Cascades, this is
What you're going to get—their very name on the map
A long walk in the rain. But it was worth it; it nearly always is:
The afternoon crying out the grief the continent had spent
All morning—all last century, so far as I can tell—trying not to
Confess. The watershed was a Japanese watercolour at risk
Of running off the canvas, the big water carrying its muted palette
Down to the sea and taking a good part of me with it. The gorge,
It turns out, is a green sermon left largely unsaid, and as we drove
Out of it, evening lay on the river like half the psalms I never knew.

Note: The Columbia River is known by many names to the people who
live along it. To the Chinook of its lower reaches, it is known as "Wimahi";
the Kwak'wala-speaking peoples of the river's middle reaches call the river
"Nch'i-Wana". Both "Wimahi" and "Nch'i-Wana" mean "the big water" or
"the big river".

MARK TREDINNICK

Waterfall

What a wonderful wasteful thing is a waterfall
that gathers the threads of a million springs
that spin them bit by bit so patiently and send them
seeping creeping weeping skeins and webs of fineness feeling
blindly down from secret hidden sources
each droplet tiny as an ant's egg merging twining into silvery fibres
streaming through the crumbs of earth and stone
with trickle tinkle music pealing through the monster forest
as though the earth itself shed tears as though the rocks themselves could bleed
sending endless tender threads of crystal tendrils
tuneful singers prayerful pilgrims in procession
mercy wrung from heart of stone
drop by drop toward the thundering great unknown

How great and glorious is the waste of waters
pouring down in tons and tons the gathered threads of brightness boiling
tangled hanks of matter weaving into tapestries of matchless pathless passion
patterns tumbling rumbling leaping stumbling seething wreathing
veils and shrouds of greyness heaving up and over boulders' blackness
lace of silver draping wrapping mossy greenness velvet sopping
mopping up the frayed the splayed the tattered foamy tatting

and gravel churning in the surge the hurling down of formless fabric
silk and satin glossy brown the billows denseness bunching folding
tumbling from the river's loom that weaves the threads the forest spun
from droplets made of molten spirit
squeezed out eased out one by one
transparent tears of mercy blood of stone

How joyous boisterous is this greatness
nothing sparing spendthrift splurging surging
roisterous waters hurling headlong lifelong hymn song
roaring whirling out and over stony ledges spouting through the river's edges
pouring down in grand abandon glassy columns crashing crushing into clouds of spray
forsaking earth but never breaking slaking thirst for godly greatness grinding fine as grit
the millstone myths of human history every second of every minute of every day
pouring down in priceless beauty spuming spewing clouds of froth and foam enduring
made of nothing never toiling timeless blameless shameless roiling waste of waters
casting down cascades of glory rising up in clouds of diamond
shouting down with chants of triumph every whisper cautious warning
rising up with life's own laughter rainbow blessings
every second of every minute of every day

EDITH SPEERS

What Gathers

Twisting stems weave
green to red against leaves
raindrop-shaped and tender,
shelter for blue-black berries.

We taste pure purple. We gather.
We touch our tongues to juice
we've asked to grow for us.

We children in our northern gardens
gather dark sweetness of saskatoons,
indigenous fruit that taught Ojibwe
beadwork patterns of vine and leaf
——winter's longing, worked by hand,
reminder of a hot day to come,
promise bright against threat.

Doubtless that was part of it:
what was gathering long ago,
the rush of other, the great change,
foods, woods, bison, prairie,
gods, songs, goods,
all about to alter.

We touch our tongues to summer.
What gathers now we do not know——
some low rumble on the globe's edge.

We gather. Nail tips and lips
stained, we do as our blood asks.
These berries the same berries
our ancestors plucked,
rolling a thumb against the curved edge,

teasing ripeness, readiness,
old ladies joking: Find me a man
can handle a woman like that!

Swoon in July sun, in sensual acts,
the fruit asks. We do as it wishes, we gather,
chilled still by long winter——
always just behind us, always just ahead.

HEID E. ERDRICH

When The Muses can't be bothered

That is when I visit their mother,
skipping past the post and wire fence,
to a house of cold milk, warm cookies made with butter.
But first, a mutual wriggle inside the non-judgmental bird-dog cage,
its muddy riot of paws, tailslap, wet kisses,
down to my best friend Billy's I-dare-ya pegleg balancing act at the rail yard,
past Charlotte's Daddy's hive-inducing tangy, Concord grapevine arbor,
onward to Mrs. Pinsky's gnarled, forgiving claw of a cherry tree,
then "the run" an arm's-length reach from the bad man's gate—
will the cops nab him this time—as they chase him half-naked down the alley?

Done! Now, flopping near the deep and pale purple iris bed
their weary mother will tend—soon as she returns from work,
pulls off her brown shoes, sighs, strokes the neighborhood tom cat,
who has straggled up to her slanted stoop, just like me,
wearing a mouse-eating grin.

I could go on, but The Muses might be listening.
They are sophisticates. Ashamed of her, with her
faded housedress, her chin wart, her birdbath, her straight path
to the trash bin of what might have been,
her shabbily asphalt-shingled house, ringed
by cheap perfume-blending, I-beam-smelting, can-lid stamping factories.
They are her fair-weather daughters,
flinging derision as they toss their glittery manes,

even as Mnemosyne rakes her silvery hair,
reaches out a steady hand,
fine tunes her radio's scratchy sound,
looks skyward for a good, hard rain.

BARBARA HOBBIE

The White Bicycle

Chained to a fence
in Paris, it suffers all winter the skinny
sleet, a white dog
in sad weather. Imagine the saucers
of such a dog's eyes; its deflated
wheels were worrisome that way, the bike
all bones, leaning soulfully,
becoming pure ghost. Where had its rider
gone? And why?
Wandering, I became proprietary,
glimpsed it again in the flea
market earrings, those pearly twins
from the forties. I couldn't afford
the bad luck of their origin; the woman
who wore them is dead.
I passed murals celebrating
the Occupation's end. Girls on bikes
in the mid-century style: skirts blown, hair
wind-caught. World breathless.
Just yesterday, a soldier pedaled past
on his Schwinn, his girlfriend
perched on the handlebars, clasping his neck,
waving to everyone they were passing.
He sang, troubadour, to her.
The white bicycle persisted,
the swanned Os of its fenders, mated
for life. Like good food, poor fool,
the booted, on foot.
I sang, Who could leave behind
a thing so fine? I sang my swell song
to a doll or a gal, in the forties' style.
Sailing anthem to keep up
the boys' spirits, You've got an angel

back home, remember.
The white bicycle became a brassiere, hitched
to a bedpost, then two Shasta daisies
in a glass on the table. Dogged and weary,
as if it had been here, like the moon's
reflection on water, or war,
or beauty, forever.

Paula Bohince

Yiu Ming Cheung

You shred daikon in winter, buckets
of crisp white you stirred with rice flour
and dried shrimp, every year preparing
turnip cake for the spring festival.

A good wife, a good mother, you followed
your husband to Thailand, even though
you both couldn't read the street signs
and on hot days your children would wash

in the city river, you followed him from Bangkok
to Hong Kong, you followed him through bankruptcy,
the night markets in Mong Kok, the nylon factory,
and then one afternoon you shut your eyes.

Maybe you expected a bodhisattva to meet you,
or an Arabian horse, but I only know the nights
when cockroaches chewed at my mother's skin,
finding the fingers she had forgotten to scrub.

You would never see Edmonton, the snow packed
roads, the salty cars, your husband floundering
in the bath tub, living with cancer, his lungs
trying to exhale the words he had learned each week:

disparate, irrupt, patina, perdurable . . .
Sundays you steeped laundry in water,
the detergent cracking your palms, cuticles
bleeding. Where is the honey in this brick?

ASHLEY CHOW

Notes on Contributors

Adil Jussawalla was born in Bombay in 1940, and went to school there. He is the author of two books of poems, *Land's End* (1962) and *Missing Person* (1976). His third book of poems, *Trying to Say Goodbye*, will be published by Almost Island Books this year.

Alina Wilson will be graduating from the University of Victoria this year with a double major in both Writing and in Germanics. After that, she intends to spend some time in Germany, working as an English teaching assistant.

Ashley Chow grew up in New Hampshire. Her poems have been published or are forthcoming in *New York Quarterly*, *Poetry International*, and *Crab Creek Review*. She is a recipient of a 2011 Robert Pinsky Global Fellowship to Timor-Leste.

Barbara Hobbie is a freelance community journalist concentrating on not-for-profit organizations. She resides in the former East Germany. Her poems have appeared in *Avant Garde*, *The Granite Review*, *Chicago Journalism Review* and *The Anthology of New England Writers*.

Barbara Myers was born and bred in Halifax, Nova Scotia, and now lives in Ottawa, Ontario. She is a contributing editor to *Arc Poetry Magazine*. Her first full collection, *Slide* (Signature Editions), came out in 2009. *Whistle For Jellyfish* (Bookland Press), of which she is one of the co-authors, has just been released.

Bronwyn Lovell is a poet and spoken word performer in Melbourne, Australia, where her poetry has been featured at several events, arts and writing festivals, as well as on local television and radio. She has a writing residency at Kinfolk Cafe, and she is a workshop facilitator for the Centre for Poetics and Justice. www.bronwynlovell.com.

Carolyn Hoople Creed teaches Creative Writing at Brandon University, Manitoba. Her writing has been published coast-to-coast in Canada, from *Prism* on the west coast to *Undertow* in the east.

C.K. Stead is a writer from New Zealand. He has published a number of novels and books of literary criticism, as well as poetry and short story collections. He was awarded a CBE in 1985 for services to New Zealand literature, and elected Fellow of the Royal Society of Literature in 1995. His *Collected Poems 1951-2006* was published in 2008 by Auckland University Press in New Zealand, and by Carcanet in the UK.

David Bunn was born in 1946. For the last three years, with wildly inadequate skills, he has been translating the French poet René Char's challenging post-war collection *Fureur et mystère*.

David Mortimer is working on a third collection of poems to follow *Red in the Morning* (Bookends, 2005) and "Fine Rain Straight Down" (*Friendly Street New Poets Eight,* Wakefield Press, 2003). Mortimer lives in Adelaide. For further information please visit the South Australian Writers' Centre website at: www.sawriters.org.au/general/david-mortimer.

Donald Givans was born in 1990 in Omagh, County Tyrone, Northern Ireland. He recently graduated with a First Class Honours Degree in English from Queen's University, Belfast, and is currently reading for a Master's at Queen's in Modern Poetry.

Edith Speers grew up in Vancouver. In 1974 she emigrated to Australia where she established herself as a widely published and prize-winning poet with two collections of verse.

Ellen Wehle's poems have appeared in Canada, Europe, the U.S. and Australia. Her first collection of poems is called *The Ocean Liner's Wake* (Shearsman, 2009). Wehle writes poetry book reviews, "a labour of love," she says, "to help bring exciting new poets to a larger audience."

Emeka Okereke is a poet from Nigeria. He is the Artistic Director of Invisible Borders Trans African Photography Initiative.

Gary Geddes has won a dozen national and international literary awards, including the Commonwealth Poetry Prize (Americas Region), the Lieutenant Governor's Award for Literary Excellence (British Columbia) and the Gabriela Mistral Prize from the Government of Chile, awarded simultaneously to Vaclav Havel, Octavio Paz, Ernesto Cardenal, Rafael Alberti and Mario Benedetti.

Heid E. Erdrich is an independent scholar, curator, playwright, and founding publisher of Wiigwaas Press, which specializes in Ojibwe-language publications. Her third poetry collection, *National Monuments*, won the 2009 Minnesota Book Award. *Cell Traffic: New and Selected Poems* is forthcoming in 2012 from University of Arizona Press.

Iain Higgins was born in Vancouver, British Columbia. His books include *Then Again* (poems), *The Invention of Poetry* (a translation of Polish poet Adam Czerniawski's Selected Poems), *The Book of John Mandeville* (a translation of a fictional medieval travel book about the East), and *Writing East: The "Travels" of Sir John Mandeville* (an academic study).

Jeff Steudel's work has appeared in several Canadian literary magazines, including *The Fiddlehead, CV2* and *Prism International*. In 2010, he received the Ralph Gustafson Poetry Prize. In 2011, his poetry was selected as a finalist in the CBC Literary Awards. He lives in Vancouver, British Columbia.

Jillian Pattinson is an Australian writer based in Melbourne. Her poems have been published in the *Australian Book Review, Griffith Review, Meanjin, Going Down Swinging, Island, Blue Dog, Poetry New Zealand, Antipodes* (U.S.A), *Quadrant, Famous Reporter, Poetrix, The Best Australian Poems 2007, Motherlode: Australian Women's Poetry 1986-2008*, and the *Newcastle Poetry Prize* anthologies.

John Wall Barger has lived in Halifax, Vancouver, Ottawa, Rome, Prague, Dublin, and Tampere. His first book of poems, *Pain-proof Men*, came out in 2009 with Palimpsest Press. His next book, *Hummingbird*, is forthcoming with Palimpsest in spring 2012.

Leslie Timmins has published poetry and short stories in numerous literary magazines. She has lived in France and Germany and now makes her home with her husband and cat a few short blocks from the sea (the sea, the sea…) in Vancouver.

Linda Rogers is a poet from Victoria, British Columbia, and the author, editor and illustrator of several dozen books of poetry, fiction and non-fiction. Currently Rogers is editing an anthology of Victoria painters and poets while tweaking a novel set in Turkey.

Margaret McCarthy's poetry and fiction have been widely published. Her most recent work appears in the online journal *Eureka Street*. Her first poetry collection is *Night Crossing* (2010). Margaret teaches professional writing and editing at Victoria University. She lives with her daughter in Melbourne, Australia.

Maria Borys was born in Poland and spent her formative years in Mexico. She writes and translates business, academic and literary texts in English, Spanish and Polish. Her work has recently been published in *Chilean Poets: A New Anthology* (Marick Press, 2010) and *Borealis: Antologia Literaria de El Dorado* (Verbum Veritas/La cita trunca, 2010).

Mark Tredinnick, an award-winning Australian poet, is the author of *Fire Diary*, *The Blue Plateau*, *The Little Red Writing Book*, and eight other works of poetry and prose. Mark lives, writes and teaches along the Wingecarribee River, southwest of Sydney. *The Lyrebird* (2011) is his most recent book of poems, and a new collection (*Body Copy*) will appear in 2012.

Mitchell Albert is a London-based book and magazine editor, born and raised in Montreal. He is also the editorial director of PEN International. Although he has fielded countless submissions of poetry, essays, short stories, articles and novels, his entry for the Montreal Prize represents the first time he has submitted his own work for a publication or prize.

Patricia Young has published ten collections of poetry. She has won many prizes including two B. C. Book Prizes for Poetry, the Pat Lowther Award for poetry, two National Magazine Awards, the League of Canadian Poets National Poetry Prize, the CBC Literary Award for Poetry, and the Arc Poem of the Year Prize. Her poems have been included in *Best Canadian Poetry in English* (Tightrope Books) in 2009, 2010 and 2011.

Paula Bohince is the author of two poetry collections, both from Sarabande Books: *Incident at the Edge of Bayonet Woods* (2008) and *The Children* (forthcoming, 2012).

Peter Richardson has published three collections of poetry with Véhicule Press in Montreal: *A Tinkers' Picnic* (1999), *An ABC of Belly Work* (2003), and *Sympathy for the Couriers* (2007), which won the QWF A.M. Klein Award for 2008. His work has appeared in *Poetry* (Chicago), *Sonora Re-*

view, *The Malahat Review*, *The Rialto* and *Poetry Ireland Review*, among others. He lives in Gatineau, Quebec.

Philip Nugent was born in London, grew up in Wiltshire and Sussex, took a degree at Edinburgh, and lived for a while in Greece where he taught English. Nugent was for many years a police officer in North London. Now he lives with his family in East Anglia.

Phillip Crymble's poems have appeared in publications around the world, including *Vallum, Arc, The Malahat Review, The Hollins Critic, Michigan Quarterly Review, Poetry Ireland Review,* and *The New York Quarterly.* Crymble now lives in Fredericton, New Brunswick, where he serves as a poetry editor for *The Fiddlehead. Not Even Laughter* (Salmon Poetry, 2012) will be his first full-length collection of poems.

Polyxeni Angelis was born in Athens, Greece. She emigrated from Greece to the U.S. with her family in 1967. She holds a Bachelor of Arts degree in Sociology from the University of Minnesota. Writing is her passion. She resides in Minnesota with her son.

Rachel Lindley has had both dramatic and light verse published in the *CBC Alberta Anthology, Margie Review, Alsop Review, Light Quarterly, Stitches,* and the anthology *Kiss and Part.* Rachel is currently working on two poetry series: *Seven Chakras for a Split Brain* and *Fair Voices: Songs in Three Rings.*

Rafi Aaron's book *Surviving the Censor—The Unspoken Words of Osip Mandelstam* (Seraphim Editions, 2006) won the Jewish Book Award for Poetry in 2007. A documentary on Rafi's poetic works entitled *The Sound Traveller,* produced by Endless Films, has aired on Bravo TV and Book Television.

Robert Wrigley teaches in the MFA program in Creative Writing at the University of Idaho. His books include *In the Bank of Beautiful Sins* (Penguin, 1995), winner of the San Francisco Poetry Center Book Award; *Reign of Snakes* (Penguin, 1999), winner of the Kingsley Tufts Award; *Lives of the Animals* (Penguin, 2003), winner of the Poets' Prize; *Earthly Meditations: New and Selected Poems* (Penguin, 2006); and most recently, *Beautiful Country* (Penguin, 2010). He is the recipient of two fellowships from the National Endowment for the Arts, as well as a fellowship from the John Simon Guggenheim Memorial Foundation. Among his other awards are the J. Howard and Barbara M. J. Wood Prize; and six Pushcart Prizes.

Ron Pretty's seventh book of poetry, *Postcards From the Centre*, was published in 2010. Until he retired in 2007, he ran the Poetry Australia Foundation and was director of Five Islands Press. He taught Creative Writing at the Universities of Wollongong and Melbourne. He has edited the literary journals *SCARP* and *Blue Dog: Australian Poetry*.

Russell Thornton's books are *The Fifth Window* (Thistledown, 2000), *A Tunisian Notebook* (Seraphim, 2002), *House Built of Rain* (Harbour, 2003), and *The Human Shore* (Harbour, 2006). He won the League of Canadian Poets National Contest in 2000 and *The Fiddlehead* magazine's Ralph Gustafson Prize in 2009. His poems have appeared in several anthologies. He now lives in North Vancouver. See: http://www.Thornton999.blogspot.com

A child of the 50s, **Shelagh McNally** grew up in Ottawa, escaped Ottawa to live in Toronto, escaped Toronto to live in Mexico on a beach, and now lives on a tiny island outside of Montreal. She has worked as a journalist and travel writer for the last 23 years.

Spencer Reece is an ordained Episcopal priest at Iglesia Catedral del Redentor in Madrid. His first book of poems, *The Clerk's Tale* (Houghton Mifflin, 2004) won the Bakeless Prize. His poems have appeared in *The New Yorker* and *Poetry* (Chicago). His forthcoming books are *The Road to Emmaus* and *The Little Entrance* (Farrar Straus Giroux, 2013).

An east-coast expatriate, **Stuart Jay Silverman** taught college in Alabama and Illinois before retiring to homes in Chicago, IL, and Hot Springs, AR. His *The Complete Lost Poems: A Selection* is published by Hawk Publishing Group. Some 400 of his poems and translations appear in journals in Canada, the U.S.A., England, and France.

Suparna Ghosh is a poet and painter based in Toronto. Her poems have been featured in various magazines and anthologies. She has exhibited her works in galleries in Toronto, New York, Mumbai and New Delhi. Ghosh's books are *Sandalwood Thoughts* and *Dots and Crosses*. See: suparnaghosh.com

Susan Glickman has published five books of poetry with Véhicule Press, most recently *Running in Prospect Cemetery: New & Selected Poems* (2004); a sixth, *The Smooth Yarrow*, is due out in 2012, the same year as her second novel, *The Tale-Teller* (Cormorant Press). Her first novel, *The Violin Lover* (2006), won the Canadian Jewish Fiction Award.

Talya Rubin is a Montreal-born, Sydney-based poet, playwright and performer. Her poetry won the Writers' Trust Bronwen Wallace Award for Emerging Writers. Her poetry, short stories and non-fiction have been published in *Grain, Matrix, Macleans Online* and *ascent* magazines.

Victor Tapner is a British poet living just outside London. He has won several poetry prizes, including the Academi Cardiff International Poetry Competition. His first full-length collection, *Flatlands* (Salt Publishing, 2010), has been shortlisted for the Seamus Heaney Centre Prize for Poetry.

Notes on Editors

Anand Thakore is a Hindustani classical vocalist by training and vocation. His first collection of verse, *Waking in December*, was published by Harbour Line. He lives in Mumbai where he teaches music privately and gives frequent public performances of his music and poetry.

Eric Ormsby has published six poetry collections. His poems have appeared in such magazines as *The New Yorker*, *The Paris Review*, and *PN Review*, and are included in *The Norton Anthology of Poetry*. An essayist and reviewer, he has also published two collections of essays on poetry and translation.

Frank M. Chipasula is a Malawian poet, editor, fiction writer and publisher of Brown Turtle Press. Chipasula is currently working on *The Burning Rose: New and (Re)Selected Poems*. He has also edited several anthologies of African poetry. His poems have been translated into French, Spanish and Chinese.

Fred D'Aguiar is a poet, novelist, playwright and essayist born in London of Guyanese parents and brought up in Guyana. His ten books of poetry and fiction have been translated into a dozen languages. Currently, he teaches at Virginia Tech where he is Gloria D. Smith Professor of Africana Studies and Professor of English. For more, see freddaguiar.com.

John Kinsella was born in Perth, Australia. His most recent books include *Activist Poetics: Anarchy in the Avon Valley* (LUP/CUP, 2010), and *Sand* (Fremantle Press, 2010). His *Peripheral Light: Selected and New Poems* (WW Norton, 2004) was selected and introduced by Harold Bloom. He is the editor of *The Penguin Anthology of Australian Poetry* (Penguin, 2009).

Michael Harris has written seven books of poetry, won several prizes, and has been published in leading journals in North America and Europe. The founding editor of Véhicule Press's Signal Editions, Harris has edited more than fifty books of poetry by over thirty-five authors. His book *Circus* (2010) was shortlisted for the Governor General's Award.

Odia Ofeimun is a Nigerian poet and political journalist. He is currently compiling the anthology, *Twentieth Century Nigerian Poetry*. Ofeimun's poems have been anthologised in many collections, including *Okike* (ed. Chinua Achebe), *Poems of Black Africa* (ed. Wole Soyinka, 1975), and *The Heinemann Book of African Poetry in English* (1990). His poetry collections include *The Poet Lied* (1980) and *A Handle for the Flutist* (1986).

Sinéad Morrissey was born and raised in Belfast. She has published four collections of poetry: *There was Fire in Vancouver* (1996), *Between Here and There* (2002), *The State of the Prisons* (2005), and *Through the Square Window* (2009), all with Carcanet Press. Her awards include The Patrick Kavanagh Award, an Eric Gregory Award, the Rupert and Eithne Strong Award, and the Michael Hartnett Poetry Prize.

Stephanie Bolster is a Canadian poet whose first book, *White Stone: The Alice Poems,* won the Governor General's Award and the Gerald Lampert Award in 1998. She has published two other poetry collections, *Two Bowls of Milk,* which won the Archibald Lampman Award, and *Pavilion.* Bolster's work has been translated into French (*Pierre Blanche: poèmes d'Alice*), Spanish, and German.

Valerie Bloom was born and grew up in Jamaica but now lives in England. She is the author of several volumes of poetry for adults and children, picture books, pre-teen and teenage novels and stories for children, and has edited a number of collections of poetry for children. Recently, Valerie Bloom was awarded an MBE for services to poetry.

Author Index

Carmine Starnino, Editor
Michael Harris, Founding Editor

THE LONG COLD GREEN EVENINGS OF SPRING Elisabeth Harvor
FAULT LINE Laura Lush
WHITE STONE: THE ALICE POEMS Stephanie Bolster
KEEP IT ALL Yves Boisvert (Translated by Judith Cowan)
THE GREEN ALEMBIC Louise Fabiani
THE ISLAND IN WINTER Terence Young
A TINKERS' PICNIC Peter Richardson
SARACEN ISLAND: THE POEMS OF ANDREAS KARAVIS David Solway
BEAUTIES ON MAD RIVER: SELECTED AND NEW POEMS Jan Conn
WIND AND ROOT Brent MacLaine
HISTORIES Andrew Steinmetz
ARABY Eric Ormsby
WORDS THAT WALK IN THE NIGHT Pierre Morency
    (Translated by Lissa Cowan and René Brisebois)
A PICNIC ON ICE: SELECTED POEMS Matthew Sweeney
HELIX: NEW AND SELECTED POEMS John Steffler
HERESIES: THE COMPLETE POEMS OF ANNE WILKINSON, 1924-1961
    Edited by Dean Irvine
CALLING HOME Richard Sanger
FIELDER'S CHOICE Elise Partridge
MERRYBEGOT Mary Dalton
MOUNTAIN TEA Peter Van Toorn
AN ABC OF BELLY WORK Peter Richardson
RUNNING IN PROSPECT CEMETERY Susan Glickman
MIRABEL Pierre Nepveu (Translated by Judith Cowan)
POSTSCRIPT Geoffrey Cook
STANDING WAVE Robert Allen
THERE, THERE Patrick Warner
HOW WE ALL SWIFTLY: THE FIRST SIX BOOKS Don Coles
THE NEW CANON: AN ANTHOLOGY OF CANADIAN POETRY
    Edited by Carmine Starnino
OUT TO DRY IN CAPE BRETON Anita Lahey
RED LEDGER Mary Dalton
REACHING FOR CLEAR David Solway
OX Christopher Patton
THE MECHANICAL BIRD Asa Boxer
SYMPATHY FOR THE COURIERS Peter Richardson
MORNING GOTHIC: NEW AND SELECTED POEMS George Ellenbogen
36 CORNELIAN AVENUE Christopher Wiseman
THE EMPIRE'S MISSING LINKS Walid Bitar
PENNY DREADFUL Shannon Stewart
THE STREAM EXPOSED WITH ALL ITS STONES D.G. Jones
PURE PRODUCT Jason Guriel
ANIMALS OF MY OWN KIND Harry Thurston
BOXING THE COMPASS Richard Greene
CIRCUS Michael Harris
THE CROW'S VOW Susan Briscoe
WHERE WE MIGHT HAVE BEEN Don Coles
MERIDIAN LINE Paul Bélanger (Translated by Judith Cowan)
THE ID KID Linda Besner
SKULLDUGGERY Asa Boxer
SPINNING SIDE KICK Anita Lahey
GIFT HORSE Mark Callanan

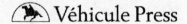 Véhicule Press